Mighty Machines
MOTORCYCLES

Ian Graham

QEB Publishing

Copyright © QEB Publishing, Inc. 2008

Published in the United States by
QEB Publishing, Inc.
23062 La Cadena Drive
Laguna Hills, CA 92653

www.qeb-publishing.com

Library of Congress Control Number: 2008010025

ISBN 978 1 59566 631 4

Printed and bound in China

Author Ian Graham
Designers Phil and Traci Morash
Editor Paul Manning
Picture Researcher Claudia Tate

Publisher Steve Evans
Creative Director Zeta Davies

Picture credits (t = top, b = bottom, c = center, l = left,
r = right, FC = front cover)
Alamy Eric Nathan 14, Steve Hamblin 15
Corbis Leo Mason 7, Marvy! 10, Richard H Cohen 18,
Tim de Waele 19, Anthony West 22 bc
Ridgeback 4
Shutterstock Digitalsport-photoagency FC,
Marcel Jancovic 1, Cornel Achirei 5, Tom Richards 8,
Keith Robinson 9, Maxim Petrichuk 11, Ravshan Mirzaitov
12, Lucian Coman 13, Maxim Petrichuk 16, Max Blain 17,
Timothy Large 20, 21, Anthony Hall, 22br

Words in **bold** can be found in the glossary on page 23.

Contents

What is a **cycle?**

Cycles are a useful way to travel around. Most cycles have two wheels that move when the rider pushes down on the pedals. A motorcycle has an engine. It can go much faster than a pedal cycle.

Pushing the pedals turns the back wheel and makes the cycle move. Squeezing the brake handles makes the cycle stop.

brake handles

pedal

There are all sorts of different motorcycles. Sports cycles and racing motorcycles are fast. **Trail** cycles are for riding off-road, on dirt tracks.

A motorcycle's engine sits under the seat in the middle of a strong frame called the chassis. A chain linked to the engine drives the back wheel.

Superbikes

A superbike is a light sports motorcycle with an incredibly powerful engine to give it extra zip. Superbikes are among the fastest cycles on the road.

Motorcycle racing is a really popular sport. Motorcycle races can be held on road tracks, special racing circuits, or off-road.

To go around corners at speed, superbike riders lean over until they almost touch the ground.

Motocross

Motocross races are held on hilly dirt tracks full of **obstacles** and jumps. The motorcycles have knobbly **tires** to grip the track.

Riders must think fast to work out the quickest way around the track. They need to be fit to take part, so they train hard.

Motocross riders jump high into the air on their cycle. They can be injured if they are thrown off the cycle at high speed.

Motocross cycles need good **suspension** and springy wheels to cushion them against bumps and jolts.

Easy riders

Harley-Davidsons are big, powerful motorcycles with lots of shiny **chrome**. They are heavy cycles, made for sitting back and cruising along the open road.

Some owners **customize** their cycles by adding extra chrome fittings and high handlebars. These cycles are sometimes called choppers, because their owners chop off the parts they do not need.

The Harley-Davidson's **exhaust** is famous for the deep, throaty roar it makes!

exhaust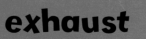

Many police forces use Harley-Davidson motorcycles because they are fast, yet also good for weaving in and out of **traffic**.

Quad bikes

A quad bike is a motorcycle with four wide wheels. It is useful for moving across soft or muddy ground without getting stuck. Many farmers use quad bikes to get around their land.

At quad sports events, riders race their bikes over all kinds of ground, from snow and ice to beaches and sandy desert.

This farmer is using a quad bike to help round up a flock of sheep.

Most quad bikes have four-wheel drive. The engine drives all four wheels. This helps the wheels to keep a grip on rough or bumpy ground.

Scooters

For zipping through busy city traffic, nothing beats a scooter. It has a smaller engine and wheels than other types of motorcycles. Instead of sitting astride the cycle, riders place their feet on a footrest between the wheels.

A motorscooter taxi whisks passengers through the busy streets of Bangkok, Thailand.

A scooter is not as fast as a motorcycle, but it is good for short journeys around town.

In Italy, a scooter is the favorite way of getting around.

Off-road cycles

Mountain cycles are made for riding off-road on rough ground. Their frames have to be stronger than ordinary cycles to stand up to jolts and knocks without getting bent or twisted.

This mountain cycle has a special frame and suspension for downhill racing.

A mountain cycle can cope with rough forest trails where no ordinary cycle can go.

Mountain cycles have fat, knobbly tires and lots of **gears** to make it easier to go up steep hills.

Racing cycles

Racing cycles are built for speed. Their tires are so thin, they hardly touch the ground.

Some racing cycles are made specially for long races along roads. Others, called track cycles, are used for indoor races in **velodromes**.

Handcycles are powered by the rider's hands instead of their feet. These racing cycles are popular with disabled riders.

Track cycles often have solid wheels that slip through the air faster than normal wheels with **spokes**.

BMX cycles

BMX stands for Bicycle Motocross. Riders tear round a circuit of bumps and jumps on a small-wheeled cycle with a single gear. BMX cycles are made for racing on hilly dirt tracks and for freestyle stunt riding.

With their small frames, fat wheels, and high handlebars, BMX cycles are great for doing tricks, such as wheelies and jumps.

BMX riders need to wear helmets and full protective gear in case of pile-ups.

Activities

- Which picture shows a cycle's saddle, handlebars, and a gear wheel?

- Make a drawing of your favorite cycle. What sort of cycle is it? Does it have big wheels or small wheels? What color is it?

- Write a story about the cycle ride you would most like to go on. It could be anywhere in the world—or even on another planet! Where would you like to go? Who would you like to meet? What do you think you might see? How long would it take?

- Which of these cycles would a racing cyclist ride?

Glossary

Chrome
A shiny coating on metal.

Customize
To alter or add to something to make it special for the owner.

Exhaust
A pipe that carries waste gases away from the engine of a cycle.

Gear
A toothed wheel that lets the pedals turn the wheels of a cycle at different speeds.

Obstacle
Something that is placed in the way of a cycle to slow it down.

Spokes
Thin, metal wires that connect the center of a bicycle wheel with the outer edge.

Suspension
A set of springs that connects a cycle's wheels and frame to give a smoother ride. The springs let the wheels follow bumps in the ground, while the rest of the cycle moves along smoothly.

Traffic
Cars, trucks, buses, and other vehicles that use the roads.

Trail
A dirt track for riding motorcycles off-road.

Tire
A rubber tube filled with air that fits around the edge of a wheel.

Velodrome
A race track specially designed for cycle racing.

Index